ANGER MANAGEMENT WORKBOOK

Dr. Barbara Thomas-Reddick, PhD, CAP

To order additional copies of this book, contact:
Xlibris
844-714-8691
www.Xlibris.com
Orders@Xlibris.com

ISBN: Softcover   978-1-6698-7984-8
              EBook   978-1-6698-7983-1

Print information available on the last page

Rev. date: 06/13/2023

Anger management:

The goal of anger management is to minimize both your feelings and emotions, the physiological awakening that anger causes. You can't get rid of, or avoid, the things or the people that antagonize you, nor can you change them, but you can learn to control your reactions. Our hope is that you learn the necessary coping skills that you need to journey in a positive direction and to maintain, sustain and manage your anger. You will learn the three types of Anger: **Passive Aggression, Open Aggression, and Assertive Aggression.** We will talk about the five stages of Anger: **Trigger, Escalation, Crisis, Recovery, and Depression. Before discussing the three types of Anger, lets assess our FEELINGS.**

Learning to recognize and express anger appropriately can make a bid difference in your life.

FEELINGS CHECK: Simply identify your feelings at this time and write it here: _____

FEELINGS CHECK-IN

 Excited

 Happy

 Surprised

 Angry

 Sad

 Scared

 Nervous

 Hurt

 Proud

TODAY I FEEL :

_____

If you identify more than one identify them here:

1.	2.	3.		
4.	5.	6.		

Take each one of the feelings you have identified and discuss what those feelings means to you.

Your Feelings:

_____

Why are you feeling this way?

_____

_____

_____

_____

What cause you to feel this way?

_____

_____

_____

What are you doing to change this feeling?

_____

_____

_____

Are you Angry?

_____

_____

_____

If you are Angry, do you know Who you are Angry with?

_____

_____

_____

How do you want to resolve this matter?

_____

_____

_____

_____

If there is someone you need to make amends, do you want to make amends?

_____

_____

_____

_____

If no, why not?

_____

_____

_____

_____

_____

(PRE) TESTING YOUR ANGER CONTROL

1. I get angry with little or no provocation.

   1   2   3   4   5

2. I have a really bad temper.

   1   2   3   4   5

3. It's hard for me to let go of thoughts that make me angry.

   1   2   3   4   5

4. When I become angry, I have urges to beat someone up.

   1   2   3   4   5

5. When I become angry, I have urges to break or tear things.

   1   2   3   4   5

6. I get impatient when people don't understand me.

   1   2   3   4   5

7. I lose my temper at least once a week.

   1   2   3   4   5

8. I embarrass family, friends, or coworkers with my anger outbursts.

   1   2   3   4   5

9. I get impatient when people in front of me drive *exactly at* the speed limit.

   1   2   3   4   5

10. 10. When my neighbors are inconsiderate, it makes me angry.

   1   2   3   4   5

11. I find myself frequently annoyed with certain friends or family.

   1   2   3   4   5

12. I get angry when people do things that they are not supposed to, like smoking in a no smoking section or having more items than marked in the supermarket express checkout line.

1   2   3   4   5

13. There are certain people who always rub me the wrong way.

1   2   3   4   5

14. I feel uptight/tense.

1   2   3   4   5

15. I yell and/or curse.

1   2   3   4   5

16. I get so angry I feel kike I am going to explode with rage.

1   2   3   4   5

17. I get easily frustrated when machines/equipment do not work properly

1   2   3   4   5

18. I remember people and situations that made me angry for a long time.

1   2   3   4   5

19. I can't tolerate incompetence. It makes me angry.

1   2   3   4   5

20. I think people try to take advantage of me.

1   2   3   4   5

TOTAL: _____

Score Key:

80-100 Your anger expression is likely getting you into serious trouble with others. It would probably be worthwhile to seek professional help.

60-80 You may not need professional help but you need to work on controlling your anger in a very deliberate manner.

50-60 You have plenty of room for improvement. Reading a self help book on anger control could be beneficial.

30-50 You're probably getting angry as often as most people. Monitor your episodes of temper and see if you can lower your score in this test in 6 months.

Below 30- Congratulate yourself. You are likely in a good comfort zone.

Passive Aggression, Open Aggression, and Assertive Aggression.

Now let's discuss the three types of Anger.

- ## Passive Aggressive

  Passive-aggressive behavior is when one person is subtly aggressive towards another. This behavior aims to punish or retaliate to a perceived slight. A person exhibiting this behavior will use passive-aggressive actions rather than communicating their dissatisfaction with words. When you have been the target of this behavior, you may not realize that a person's hostility was purposeful. You may be left wondering why the person treated you poorly. Was it an accident? Are you being too sensitive?

- What are some of the reason people behave passively aggressively?

  1. Most of the time individuals use passive-aggressive behavior for different reasons. A person may not typically behave this way, but occasionally they will exhibit this behavior. According to Clinical Studies & Dr. Barbara Thomas-Reddick, there are reasons why people act this way.

     - We are taught showing anger is intolerable.
     - Cover up or sugarcoated angry responses are welcome.
     - Aggressiveness is harder.
     - Trouble Free to rationalize behavior.
     - Getting Even feels superior.
     - Advantageous
     - Feel effective.

- Examples of Passive-Aggressive Behavior

  Stubbornness, procrastination, and a get back behavior are typically exhibited. A person may false-face their anger by making excuses for their non-receptiveness. People who are confrontational or aggressive may deny being angry even though it is obvious that they are upset. A procrastinating passive-aggressive co-worker may wait until the last minute to complete their assigned work or submit work late as a means of getting back.

- **Passive Aggressive Speech**

  There are common ways that people speak to show their hidden unkindness. You may notice that the way they are talking to you doesn't quite make sense and that you are getting frustrated. According to clinical studies, passive-aggressive people may say:

  - "I'm okay."
  - "I'm not angry."
  - "Okay"
  - "Anyway"

- "I thought you knew."
- "I'd be delighted to."
- "I was only playing."
- "Why are you mad?"

• Open Aggressive

Open aggression is a sharp contrast to passive-aggressive anger, as it's usually expressed outwardly---- mostly in a physically or verbally aggressive way. People who express outward anger often do so with the of hurting others or destroying things to retaliate for acts they perceived were wrongfully done to them.

Many people tend to lash out in anger and rage, becoming physically or verbally aggressive and can often times hurt themselves or others. Open Aggression comes out in bullying, blackmailing, accusing, shouting, bickering, sarcasm, fighting, and criticism.

How to control your anger

1. Count to 10. Counting to 10 gives you time to cool down, so you can think more clearly and overcome the impulse to lash out.
2. Breathe slowly. ...
3. Inhale and Exhale
4. Exercise can help with anger. ...
5. Looking after yourself may keep you calm. ...
6. Get creative. ...
7. Talk about how you feel. ...
8. Anger management programs.
9. Meditation/Yoga/Prayer/Read a Book etc.

• Assertive Agressive

Assertive anger: This is usually the best way to communicate feelings of anger because anger is expressed directly and in a nonthreatening way to the person involved. A statement such as "I feel angry when you ..." is an example of assertive anger.

We will talk about the five stages of Anger: Trigger, Escalation, Crisis, Recovery, and Depression.

Trigger:

Everyone has their own triggers for what makes them angry, but some common ones include situations in which we feel:

- Threatened or attacked.
- Frustrated or powerless
- Like we're being invalidated or treated unfairly
- Like people are not respecting our feelings or possessions.

Start by considering these 10 anger management tips.

a. **Think before you speak.**
b. **Once you're calm, express your concerns.**
c. **Get some exercise.**
d. **Identify possible solutions.**
e. **Stick with "I" statements.**
f. **Don't hold a grudge.**
g. **Use humor to release tension.**

Escalation:

Escalation. In this process, the escalation phase involves cues that indicate anger is building. As stated in the introduction to anger management, these cues can be physical, behavioral, emotional, or cognitive (thoughts). As you may recall, cues are warning signs, or responses, to anger-provoking events.

The Four-Step Verbal De-Escalation Process

- Step 1: Recognize and Assess the Situation. Your safety is paramount. ...
- Step 2: Respond Calmly. Human beings tend to mimic each other's behavior, so don't respond with anger, sarcasm, or inflexibility. ...
- Step 3: Listen with Empathy. ...
- Step 4: Validate and Show Respect.

Crisis:

The crisis phase involves the young person behaving in an aggressive manner, either physically or verbally, towards another person, an object or themselves. This may include shouting, throwing, or hitting an object and or striking a person.

Recovery:

Recovery is the physiological and psychological wind down phase that returns a young person to a pre-angry state. This slow cool down process can take from less than an hour to days, depending on the intensity and length of the anger-related episode.

Depression:

People with depressive illness often have symptoms of overt or suppressed anger.

Can depression make you have anger issues?

Those with anger traits face exaggerated problem during symptomatic period of depression. Pharmacological management helps in control of depressive and anxiety symptoms, but rarely addresses anger symptoms.

Dealing with someone else's Anger:

Here are some tips:

Keep your cool. Don't answer anger with anger. Remember that anger can lead people to say things they don't really mean. Criticism, threats, or name-calling won't help resolve the situation. Don't take it personally. Try to understand why the person is angry. His or her feelings may have little or nothing to do with you. Listen to the person. Sometimes an angry person just needs to "blow off steam". Let the person express his or her feelings. Don't interrupt. Maintain eye contact to show you are listening. Think of solutions together. If you're having a conflict with someone, try to find solutions that you can both agree on. Do this only when you are both calm.

Some Common causes of anger include, but not limited to:

1. **Stress:** Stress related to work, family, health, and money problems may make you feel anxious and irritable.

2. **Frustration/Resentment:** You may get angry if you fail to reach a goal or feel as if things are out of your control.

3. **Anxiety/Fear:** Anger is a natural response to threats of violence or to physical or verbal abuse.

4. **Aggravation/Annoyance:** You may reach in anger to minor irritations and daily hassles.

5. **Sadness/Disappointment:** Anger often results when expectations and desires aren't met.

6. **Bitterness/Resentment:** You may feel angry when you've been hurt, rejected, or offended.

MAKING AMENDS

Credit to Nick https://www.amethystrecovery.org

As to Nick writing with Amethyst recovery & the Holistic Plan of Care Program believes that MAKING AMENDS is a vital part of an individual's life. When one understands the proper steps in how to make amends with people, they have either hurt or caused discomfort too, this allows one to fill the voids. Studies has proven that when an individual suffers with addictions one of the 12 steps that every Alcoholic Anonymous or Drug Disorder member needs to complete is rekindling with loved ones, family and friends. Not only does making amends help you get over past mistakes, but it also helps repair your relationships with other people. However, some people are afraid of making amends because they don't know what to say, how to start, or how others are going to respond. While everyone's journey is different, and you cannot control how others will respond, there are ways to approach this step appropriately.

Start With a Thoughtful Apology

When you make amends, you must apologize for the hurt and pain you caused. Keep in mind, it doesn't have to be a lengthy apology; it just needs to be honest. Some things you can open with include:

- I'm sorry.
- I feel bad about what I did.
- I'm sorry I made myself sick.
- I'm sorry for what I've put you through.
- I know this has been hard on both of us.

Take Responsibility for Your Actions

Don't deny responsibility for the harm you've caused, even if you think it was someone else's fault or the victim brought it to themselves. When making amends, owning the responsibility for your actions can sound like:

- I recognize I am powerless against drinking, or I recognize I am powerless against drugs.
- I accept responsibility for what I did.
- I know that I caused you harm.
- I acknowledge that I ignored your help.
- I realize that my actions were hurtful.

Admit What You Did Wrong

One of the most important parts of making amends is being specific about what you did wrong. Rather than saying something vague like, "I'm sorry for being rude to you," say something like, "When you were trying to introduce yourself at that party, I interrupted and made inappropriate comments, and I apologize for my behavior. Please accept my apology."

Don't try to justify what happened either; simply admit that your actions were wrong without explaining why they occurred in the first place. One way to recognize what you did wrong is by saying things like:

- I was wrong.
- I did this and I take full responsibility for my actions.
- This was my fault.

Genuinely Feel Remorse

It is important to genuinely feel remorse for the person you hurt, what you did, and the pain you caused. The person or people affected by your behavior are not even there in this room with you, so their feelings and reactions must come from within you. You need to be able to convey genuine feelings of remorse to make amends successfully.

Ask for Forgiveness

When asking for forgiveness, you must be sincere. This means that you are willing to accept the consequences of your actions. You also need to be ready to make amends and change your behavior in the future. If someone has forgiven you and is willing to accept your apology but continues to treat you poorly or speak badly about you to others, it's okay not to go back into their lives right away—but do try again eventually. Forgiveness works both ways, and sometimes, even though a person says they forgive you, they might not be ready to mean it yet.

Ask What You Can Do to Amend Your Wrongdoing

While it may seem like a simple question, the "What can I do?" question is more of a two-part query: First, you're asking permission to make amends. Second, what they say after they tell you what they need from you determines whether or not your apology has been accepted.

This is an important part of making amends because it shows that you're taking ownership of your actions. It lets others know that you're not going to repeat the same mistakes repeatedly by offering them a way to avoid having to deal with your apologies every week or two.

Be Patient and Persistent

If you're looking to make amends with a loved one or family member, you must take the time to develop a plan. You'll also want to be mindful of your intention and follow through on it consistently over time.

It can sometimes feel like an uphill battle when trying not just to apologize but also to make amends for past mistakes. But remember: the most important thing is that you do what's best for yourself and your relationship with this person in the long run, even if it takes smaller steps at first. So don't be afraid of asking for help from others in AA who might have more experience in this area than you.

It's important to remember that making amends is a process. You can't expect everything to go perfectly when you try to do it for the first time but keep trying. And even though you might still make some mistakes along the way, don't let them discourage you from making amends in future situations where appropriate.

(A Self Awareness Model)

WHO ARE YOU?

NAME

DEMOGRAPHIC

Hopefully by now, you have read Dr. Barbara Reddick's book, The Presence of a Chaplain & My Personal Tapestry of Life. If you have not, we encourage you to also read as well.

This section will allow you to look at self to become aware of who you are and who you may want to become. Please read each question carefully and explain in detail your thoughts, feelings, concerns, and observations.

Please understand that this is your personal tapestry of life and only you will read it unless you decide to share as I have. The journey in this student handbook will hopefully allow you to become empowered with your self-awareness. Work at your own pace, realizing that you can stop and start at any time.

(If you feel uncomfortable answering any of the questions, move on to the next question until you complete it. At the end of the journey, you may feel comfortable revisiting the unanswered questions.)

NAME:

DATE:

TIME:

AGE:

✓ EDUCATION

7th	8th	9th	10th	11th	12th	1 yr. ollege	2 yrs. college	3 yrs. college	4 yrs. college	5 yrs. college	6 yrs. college

Male: _____

Female: _____

✓ Please (How many children do you have?)

- Married   Children: 1-2   3-4   5-6   7-8   9-10
- Divorce
- Single
- Dating
- Student

Share how you are feeling at this moment. (In detail)

_____

_____

_____

_____

_____

_____

_____

_____

_____

_____

_____

_____

_____

_____

_____

_____

_____

_____

Do you have a clue of what you would like to learn about yourself?
YES _____   NO _____

Explain what you would like to learn about YOU?

_____

_____

_____

_____

_____

_____

_____

_____

_____

What is your favorite food? _____		

What is your favorite food? _____

What is your favorite game you like to play? _____

What do you like to do? _____

Who is your favorite Artist? _____

What grade are you presently in? _____

What is your favorite sport? _____

If you could meet a celebrity, who would you choose?_____

WHO RAISED YOU?

Mother	Father	Grandma	Grandpa	Sister	Brother	Auntie
Other Family	Uncle	Pastor	Friends	Neighbors	Teacher	Cousin or Other

WHAT IS YOUR FAVORITE COLOR?

Do you have a pet, if so, share the name?

_____

_____

_____

_____

_____

_____

If you have a pet, describe the level of care you provide for your pet.

_____

_____

_____

How many pets have you had in your lifetime? _____

From a scale from 1 to 10, how would you number yourself as the level of care for pets? A scale from 1-10 1---don't care at all for pets 10--- care a whole lot

Do you attend church?
YES _____   NO ____   _____Never

If you attend church, temple, or synagogue? What is your denomination?

_____

_____

_____

What do you like about your church, temple, or synagogue?

_____

_____

_____

What would like to be when you grow up?

_____

_____

_____

How many siblings do you have? (circle)

1	2	3	4	5	6	7	8	9	10

How many stepsisters or step brothers do you have?

1	2	3	4	5	6	7	8	9	10

Do you like school? If yes, explain why? If no, explain why?

_____

_____

_____

_____

_____

_____

_____

_____

_____

If you like school, explain in detail what you like about school and why?

_____

_____

_____

_____

_____

_____

_____

_____

While growing up who raised you? Explain this experience.

_____
_____
_____

_____
_____
_____

_____
_____
_____

Are you okay with who raised you? If yes explain, if no explain.

_____
_____
_____

_____
_____
_____

_____
_____
_____

How was your upbringing? Explain

_____
_____
_____

_____
_____
_____

_____

_____

_____

_____

_____

_____

_____

_____

_____

_____

_____

Paint the picture in words how you would like for your family to look.

_____

_____

_____

_____

_____

_____

_____

_____

If you could change one thing about your family lifestyle, what would it be?

_____

_____

_____

_____

_____

_____

_____

_____

_____

_____

Are you being raised by both parents, single parent, or no parent, etc.?
Explain

_____

_____

_____

_____

_____

_____

_____

Which parent do you feel comfortable to share your deep thoughts with?
Mom   Dad   Other

Who is your favorite teacher and why?

_____
_____
_____

_____
_____

_____
_____

_____

What is it you like(d) about this teacher?

_____
_____

_____

If you could change one thing in your school, what would it be?

_____
_____

_____

_____
_____

_____

_____

Do you like your school that you are presently attending?

_____
_____

_____

If your answer is yes, explain what you like about your school.

YES_____

_____

_____

_____

_____

_____

_____

_____

If your answer is no, explain what you do not like about your school.

_____

_____

_____

_____

_____

_____

_____

_____

While growing up, did you spend time with grandma and grandpa?

_____

_____

_____

_____

_____

_____

_____

_____

If you spent time with either, explain how you felt then and now?

_____

_____

_____

_____

_____

_____

_____

_____

If you did not spend time with your grandparents, how do you feel about this?

_____

_____

_____

_____

_____

_____

_____

_____

Do you feel that there are benefits for children who have grandparents in their lives? If so, why? If not, why?

_____

_____

_____

_____

_____

Make an observation of how you are feeling NOW.

_____

_____

_____

_____

_____

_____

_____

_____

Do you feel that this student handbook is helping you thus far?
YES _____   NO _____

What do you enjoy doing when you have free time?

_____

_____

_____

What are your strengths?

_____

_____

_____

What are your weaknesses?

_____

_____

_____

If you could change one thing about you, what would it be and why?

_____

_____

_____

_____

_____

_____

_____

_____

If there is something you could change, do you feel that this has hindered you from moving forward in your life?

_____

_____

_____

_____

_____

_____

_____

_____

_____

_____

_____

_____

_____

_____

Do you feel that life hasn't been fair?

YES _____   NO _____

EXPLAIN:

_____

_____

_____

_____

_____

_____

_____

_____

_____

_____

_____

_____

_____

_____

_____

_____

_____

_____

_____

_____

_____

_____

If you feel that life for you hasn't been fair, identify one thing you can do to move things forward in a positive manner.

_____

_____

_____

_____

_____

_____

_____

_____

Name one thing that you really dislike for someone to say or do to you?

_____

_____

_____

_____

_____

_____

_____

Is there someone you are angry with?

_____

_____

_____

_____

_____

_____

If there is someone you are angry with, why?

_____

_____

_____

_____

_____

_____

Have you tried to resolve this matter?
YES _____   NO _____

If the matter is not resolved, do you want to resolve this matter? If yes, how do you plan on putting this behind you?

_____

_____

_____

_____

_____

_____

_____

_____

_____

ACTIVITY

TAKE TIME TO WRITE A LETTER TO SOME ONE
YOU WANT TO MAKE AMENDS WITH!
THERE MAY BE MORE THAN ONE PERSON.
US THE NEXT FORMAT or YOU CAN USE YOUR PAPER.

FROM: _____

_____

_____

TO:_____

_____

_____

Dear _____:

_____

_____

_____

_____

_____

_____

_____

_____

_____

_____

_____

_____

_____

_____

_____

_____

_____

_____

_____

_____

_____

_____

_____

_____

_____

_____

_____

_____

_____

Sincerely,

TAKE A BREAK!!!!!!!
Debrief

Self-Care

Embrace the moment of your true feelings and know that if you are feeling angry, mad, happy, sad, or anxious, it's okay. Name and claim your true feelings.

Examples of taking a break:

1. Take a walk!
2. Drink a cup of coffee or hot tea etc.
3. Inhale/Exhale
4. Yoga/Exercise
5. Meditation/Prayer
6. Self-Care
7. Sing a Melody

WELCOME BACK!!!!!!

TAKE AN OBSERVATION OF HOW YOU ARE FEELING AT THIS TIME.

_____
_____
_____
_____
_____
_____
_____
_____
_____
_____
_____
_____
_____
_____
_____
_____
_____
_____
_____
_____
_____
_____

External and Internal Alterations

Have you ever used drugs?
Yes _____ **No** _____

Have you ever used alcohol?
Yes _____ **No** _____

If yes, what type of drug(s) have you ever used? (CHECK Yes or NO)

SUBSTANCE	YES	NO
Alcohol		
Cannabis		
Crack Cocaine		
Cocaine		
Heroin		
Molly		
Methamphetamine		
LSD		
Flakka		
OTHER		

If not, explain on a separate sheet of paper, sharing a moment in your life where you wanted to use but didn't.

_____

_____

_____

_____

_____

_____

What kept you from using it?

_____

_____

_____

_____

_____

_____

Share this experience of how this make you feel that you were able to not use drugs or alcohol.

_____

_____

_____

_____

_____

_____

Please explain the age you started using drugs. _____

Who introduced drugs to you? _____

How do you feel about this person today? Explain where you met this person and how you met this individual in detail.

_____

_____

_____

_____

_____

_____

_____

_____

_____

Did you trust this person at the time he or she introduced this drug to you?

_____
_____
_____
_____
_____
_____
_____
_____
_____
_____

What would you do differently if you could turn back the hands of time?

_____
_____
_____
_____
_____
_____
_____
_____
_____
_____
_____
_____

How do you feel about leaders?

_____
_____
_____

_____
_____
_____

_____
_____

_____
_____
_____

How do you feel a leader should lead?

_____
_____
_____

_____
_____

_____
_____

_____
_____

_____
_____

_____

If you attend church, temple, or synagogue, how do you feel about your pastor, rabbi, or priest, etc.?

_____

_____

_____

_____

_____

_____

_____

_____

_____

_____

Does your pastor, rabbi, priest, etc., exemplify good leadership skills?

_____

_____

_____

_____

_____

_____

_____

_____

_____

_____

_____

If not, identify the areas you would like your leader to improve in.

_____

_____

_____

_____

_____

_____

_____

_____

_____

Define leadership.

_____

_____

_____

_____

_____

_____

_____

_____

_____

_____

_____

How do you feel about this overall observation of self and others?

_____

_____

_____

_____

_____

_____

_____

_____

_____

_____

_____

_____

_____

_____

_____

_____

Would you recommend this workbook to someone else?
Yes _____   No _____

GREAT WORK!!! YOU DESERVE A PAT ON THE BACK. I look forward to speaking with you in the near future. We can arrange for a conference call, if you'd like.

Dr. Barbara Thomas-Reddick

WHEN YOU DO NOT KNOW WHO YOU ARE, YOU WILL BE WHAT OTHERS WANT YOU TO BE!!!

"WHO ARE YOU?"

_____

_____

_____

WHEN YOU COMPLETE YOUR HANDBOOK, IN ORDER TO RECEIVE YOUR CERTIFICATE OF COMPLETION, CONTACT our office Manager at 850-201-7105 Office/ 850-201-7101 Fax or email me at **Holisticplanofcare@gmail.com**

IF YOU WOULD LIKE TO BOOK DR. BARBARA THOMAS- REDDICK FOR FUTURE ENGAGEMENTS FEEL FREE TO CONTACT ME AT THE NUMBER ABOVE or at 850-662-4873

WEBSITES:
www.thepresenceofachaplain.com
WWW.HPOCARE.ORG
www.ifgoddontdoit.com

Stay focused for upcoming books.

LET'S TAKE A POST ANGER TEST AND COMPARE THE TWO.

(POST) TESTING YOUR ANGER CONTROL

1. I get angry with little or no provocation.
   1   2   3   4   5

2. I have a really bad temper.
   1   2   3   4   5

3. It's hard for me to let go of thoughts that make me angry.
   1   2   3   4   5

4. When I become angry, I have urges to beat someone up.
   1   2   3   4   5

5. When I become angry, I have urges to break or tear things.
   1   2   3   4   5

6. I get impatient when people don't understand me.
   1   2   3   4   5

7. I lose my temper at least once a week.
   1   2   3   4   5

8. I embarrass family, friends, or coworkers with my anger outbursts.
   1   2   3   4   5

9. I get impatient when people in front of me drive *exactly at* the speed limit.
   1   2   3   4   5

10. When my neighbors are inconsiderate, it makes me angry.
    1   2   3   4   5

11. I find myself frequently annoyed with certain friends or family.
    1   2   3   4   5

12. I get angry when people do things that they are not supposed to, like smoking in a no smoking section or having more items than marked in the supermarket express checkout line.

    1   2   3   4   5

13. There are certain people who always rub me the wrong way.

    1   2   3   4   5

14. I feel uptight/tense.

    1   2   3   4   5

15. I yell and/or curse.

    1   2   3   4   5

16. I get so angry I feel like I am going to explode with rage.

    1   2   3   4   5

17. I get easily frustrated when machines/equipment do not work properly

    1   2   3   4   5

18. I remember people and situations that made me angry for a long time.

    1   2   3   4   5

19. I can't tolerate incompetence. It makes me angry.

    1   2   3   4   5

20. I think people try to take advantage of me.

    1   2   3   4   5

TOTAL: _____

Score Key:

80-100 Your anger expression is likely getting you into serious trouble with others. It would probably be worthwhile to seek professional help.

60-80 You may not need professional help, but you need to work on controlling your anger in a very deliberate manner.

50-60 You have plenty of room for improvement. Reading a self-help book on anger control could be beneficial.

30-50 You're probably getting angry as often as most people. Monitor your episodes of temper and see if you can lower your score in this test in 6 months.

Below 30- Congratulate yourself. You are likely in a good comfort zone.

Final Test for completion:

1. **Who is the Professor for this class?**
   a. Joyce Melanie
   b. Dr. Roy Lee
   c. Dr. Barbara Thomas-Reddick

2. **Define Anger**
   a. a strong feeling of annoyance, displeasure, or hostility
   b. Anger can be a good thing. It can give you a way to express negative feelings, for example, or motivate you to find solutions to problems.
   c. It is okay to be angry, it is what you do with it.
   d. All above

3. **Write down the three types of Anger?**
   1. _____
   2. _____
   3. _____

4. **Learning to recognize and express anger appropriately can make a bid difference in your life. (CHECK your answer)**
   _____TRUE OR _____FALSE

5. **The Five Stages of Anger.**
   a. _____   b. _____
   c. _____   d. _____
   e. _____

6. **What are some of the drugs on the streets now?**
   1. _____   2. _____   3. _____
   4. _____   5. _____

7. **Name two of the steps in MAKING AMENDS?**

   a. _____

   b. _____

8. **Is it okay to become Angry? _____yes or _____no**

9. **If one becomes angry, what is one approach that one could take and not harm self or anyone else?**

   _____

   _____

   _____

10. **From 1-10, one being the calmest and ten being the angriest, which number would you assess yourself as? Please cirlce**

   1   2   3   4   5   6   7   8   9   10

AFTER YOU HAVE COMPLETED THE CLASS WITH A 70% or higher, YOU WILL RECEIVE A CERTIFICATE OF COMPLETION IN YOUR EMAIL. SIGNED BY A CERTIFIED ADDICTION PROFESSIONAL.

Dr. B. Thomas Reddick

Printed in the United States
by Baker & Taylor Publisher Services